Fathers
are
Forever

Dr. Criswell Freeman

WG
WALNUT GROVE PRESS
NASHVILLE, TN

Fathers

are
Forever

Dr. Criswell Freeman

Walnut Grove Press
Nashville, TN 37203

2nd Edition
ISBN 1-58334-135-8

The ideas expressed in this book are not, in all cases, exact quotations, as some have been edited for clarity and brevity. In all cases, the author has attempted to maintain the speaker's original intent. In some cases, material for this book was obtained from secondary sources, primarily print media. While every effort was made to ensure the accuracy of these sources, the accuracy cannot be guaranteed. For additions, deletions, corrections or clarifications in future editions of this text, please write Walnut Grove Press.

Printed in the United States of America
Cover & Page Layout Design by Bart Dawson
Cover Photo: www.comstock.com
1 2 3 4 5 6 7 8 9 10 • 02 03 04 05 06 07 08 09 10

Acknowledgments: The author is indebted to Angela Freeman, Dick and Mary Freeman, Ron Smith, Jim Gallery, and to the creative staff at Walnut Grove Press.

For Dad

Table of Contents

Introduction

You hold in your hands a simple tribute to fathers.
On these pages, you will examine the attributes of dynamic dads and peerless pops. You will consider the skills of fabulous fathers and great granddads. And, you will discover a heaping helping of fatherly advice.

This collection of quotations celebrates the paternal side of parenting, and with good cause. Fathers bequeath a timeless legacy—one that is passed from generation to generation. The hand that rocks the cradle also places its handprint upon eternity. A father's love lasts a lifetime—and beyond.

If you happen to be a father, and since you're reading this book there is a high probability that you are, congratulations and thank you. In touching the lives of your children and their friends, you have left the world a better place. Your handiwork will endure...forever.

Chapter 1
A Father Is...

No music is so pleasant to
my ears as that word—
father.

—

Lydia Maria Child

The dictionary defines father as "a male parent," but every grateful son or daughter knows that such a concise definition is woefully incomplete. A good father is many things: He is a leader, a provider, an advisor, a disciplinarian, a teacher, a coach, a recreation director, a friend, a spiritual guide, a baby-sitter, a transportation director, a handyman, a physician, and a banker.

To a young child, a father is an all-purpose, all-powerful, all-knowing figure. As the child matures and the teenage years reach full bloom, the father's image may become tarnished—temporarily. But, the adult child, armed with a better understanding of the demands of parenthood, is likely to appreciate his or her father more than ever. And rightly so.

On the pages that follow, we consider the wide-ranging implications of fatherhood, a job so demanding and so important that God reserved it for that great fraternity of homeplace heroes: our dads.

There is no more vital calling or vocation
                    for men than fathering.

—John R. Throop

A father is the man who expects his son to be
                    as good as the man he meant to be.

—Franklin A. Clark

One father equals a hundred schoolmasters.

—George Herbert

A father provides love, strength, wisdom, security,
example, friendship, and fun.

—*Jim Gallery*

Children's children are the crown of old men;
the glory of children are their fathers.

—*Proverbs 17:6 KJV*

Tell me who your father is and I'll tell you who you are.

—*Philippine Proverb*

The quality of a child's relationship with his or her father seems to be one of the most important influences in deciding how that person will react to the world.

—

John Nicholson

You are a king by your own fireside,
    as much as any monarch in his thrown.
                                    —*Miguel de Cervantes*

A father is a banker provided by nature.
                                    —*French Proverb*

The most important thing a father can do
    for his children is to love their mother.
                                    —*Rev. Theodore M. Hesburgh*

A father is a man who can't get on the phone,
    in the bathroom, or out of the house.
                                    —*Anonymous*

When I was a boy of 14, my father was so ignorant I could hardly stand to have the old man around. But, when I got to be 21, I was astonished at how much the old man had learned in only seven years.

—

Mark Twain

Raising Our Children

Every child is a priceless gift from the Father above. With that gift comes immense responsibility. Wise parents understand the critical importance of raising their children with love, with family, with discipline, and with faith.

It has been said, quite correctly, that our children are on loan from God. It might be added that the term of that loan is all too brief. In the blink of an eye—or so it seems—our babies are grown and gone. Thus, each day that we spend with our children is indeed a gift...but a gift with a definite time limit. May we, as parents, use that time wisely.

Have we not all one father? Did not one God create us?

—

Malachi 2:10 NIV

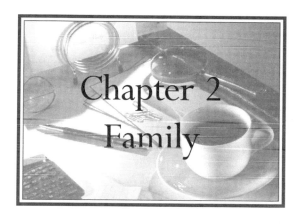

Chapter 2
Family

A happy family is but an earlier heaven.

—

Sir John Bowring

Sam Levenson joked, "Insanity is hereditary, you can get it from your kids." Spoken like a man with a big family.

An anonymous parent once observed, "A loving family is a thing of beauty and a *job* forever." Unfortunately, this statement is only partially true. Parenting is, of course, a job, but the work of raising our children is not "forever"; it is temporary. Still, we can be comforted in the knowledge that *the fruits* of our parental labors, our children (and their children), outlive us just as surely as our children influence the world in ways that we can never fully comprehend.

The philosopher George Santayana wrote, "A family is a masterpiece of nature." In this chapter, we consider that masterpiece...and its master, dear old Dad.

A family is a place where principles are hammered
and honed on the anvil of everyday living.
—*Charles R. Swindoll*

A home is a place where we find direction.
—*Gigi Graham Tchividjian*

Money can build or buy a house. Add love to that,
and you have a home. Add God to that,
and you have a temple.
—*Anne Ortland*

No man can possibly know what life means,
what the world means, what anything means,
until he has a child and loves it.
—*Lafcadio Hearn*

Other things may change us, but we start
and end with the family.

—*Anthony Brandt*

Upon our children—how they are taught—
rests the fate, or fortune, of tomorrow's world.

—*B. C. Forbes*

A family is a unit composed not only of children,
but of men, women, an occasional
animal, and the common cold.

—*Ogden Nash*

It takes a heap of lovin' in a house to make it a home.

—*Edgar A. Guest*

You don't choose your family. They are God's gift
to you, as you are to them.

—*Desmond Tutu*

There are three partners in any man:
God, his father, and his mother.

—*Old Saying*

Blessed indeed is the man who hears many
gentle voices call him father!

—*Lydia Maria Child*

A child is the greatest poem ever known.

—*Christopher Morley*

A family is the first and essential cell of human society.

—*Pope John XXIII*

When the family is together, the soul is at peace.

—*Russian Proverb*

A family is the school of duties founded on love.

—*Felix Adler*

A large family gives beauty to the house.

—Indian Proverb

A family divided against itself will perish together.

—Indian Proverb

The family you come from isn't as important
as the family you're going to have.

—Ring Lardner

Father and mother are the most precious jewels on earth.

—Philippine Proverb

Children have more need of models than critics.

—Joseph Joubert

The family is the nucleus of civilization.

—Will and Ariel Durant

Lucky is that man whose children make
his happiness in life.

—Euripides

Creating a warm, caring, supportive, encouraging
environment is probably the most important thing
you can do for your family.

—Stephen Covey

A baby is God's opinion that the world should go on.

—*Carl Sandburg*

A child is a beam of sunlight from
the Infinite and Eternal.

—*Lyman Abbott*

A torn jacket is soon mended, but hard words
bruise the heart of a child.

—*Henry Wadsworth Longfellow*

It is a wise father that knows his own child.

—*William Shakespeare*

A father's interest in having a child—
perhaps his only child—may be unmatched
by any other interest in his life.

—*William H. Rehnquist*

About his children every parent is blind.

—*Old Saying*

Build me a son, O Lord, who will be strong enough
to know when he is weak and brave enough
to face himself when he is afraid.

—*Douglas MacArthur*

We can either grace our children, or damn them
with unrequited wounds which never seem to heal.
Men, as fathers, you have such power.

—R. Kent Hughes

They say the best product off a farm is the children.

—Earl Simpson

All children alarm their parents, if only because
you are forever expecting to encounter yourself.

—Gore Vidal

When a father helps a son, both smile;
when a son must help his father, both cry.

—Old Jewish Saying

What we desire our children to become,
      we must endeavor to be before them.

—*Andrew Combe*

A good father will leave his imprint
      on his daughter for the rest of her life.

—*James C. Dobson*

When brothers agree, no fortress is so strong
      as their common life.

—*Antisthenes*

In a big family, the first child is kind of like
      the first pancake. If it's not perfect, that's okay,
            there are a lot more coming along.

—*Antonin Scalia*

To be successful in the family, the father must have
the welfare of each family member at heart,
and his decisions and plans must be based upon
what is best for them.

—*Helen Andelin*

America's future will be determined by the home
and the school. The child becomes largely what he
is taught; hence we must watch what we teach
and how we live.

—*Jane Addams*

When I met Michael Jordan I wondered how,
with all the distractions, he could maintain such
mountains of freshness. Then I met his family
and I understood. It sounds corny,
but it's true—love shows.

—*Doug Collins*

Our sages recommended that a father
    should spend less than his means on food,
    up to his means on dress, and beyond
    his means for his wife and children.

                     —*Maimonides*

It is not enough for parents to understand children.
    They must accord children the privilege of
    understanding *them*.

                     —*Milton R. Sapirstein*

There is a balance between firmness and tenderness
    that good fathers constantly try to achieve.

                     —*Steve Farrow*

It is better to keep children to their duty by a
    sense of honor and by kindness than by fear.

                     —*Terence*

My mother gave me my religious training
and my respect for discipline. My father supplied the
athletic genes. There is nothing that I am today that I
would be without family.

—*Emmitt Smith*

A man cannot leave a better legacy to the world
than a well-educated family.

—*Thomas Scott*

Here all mankind is equal: rich and poor alike,
they love their children.

—*Euripides*

Children are the hands by which we take hold of heaven.

—*Henry Ward Beecher*

Raising children is not unlike a long distance race in
which the contestants must learn to pace themselves.
That is the secret of winning.

—*James C. Dobson*

Honor your father-in-law and mother-in-law,
for now they are your parents.

—*The Book of Tobit*

Govern a family as you would cook a small fish—
very gently.

—*Chinese Proverb*

Through the survival of their children, happy parents are
able to think calmly, and with a very practical
affection, of a world in which they are
to have no direct share.

—*Walter Pater*

The debt of gratitude we owe our mother
and father goes forward, not backward.
What we owe our parents is the bill presented
to us by our children.

—*Nancy Friday*

The voice of parents is the voice of gods, for
to their children they are heaven's lieutenants.

—*William Shakespeare*

There is no grandfather who does not adore his grandson.

—*Victor Hugo*

The father in praising the son extols himself.

—*Chinese Proverb*

Your Family:
A Priceless Gift

Your most prized earthly possession is not your home, your car, or your savings account. Your most prized earthly possession is, of course, your family. Your family is a priceless gift from heaven above: treasure it, protect it, support it, and, above all, love it.

As a father, your responsibilities are profound; so are your rewards. Today and every day, give thanks for your clan, and then demonstrate your gratitude by serving up a heaping helping of laughter and leadership. Each day with your family is another blessing from God. Treasure the gift.

Home is the place where
the great are small and
the small are great.

—

Robert Savage

Chapter 3
Fatherly Advice

Whoever teaches his son
teaches not only his son
but also his son's son.

—

The Talmud

A hundred years before the birth of Christ, Publilius Syrus observed, "Many receive advice, few profit from it." For twenty-one centuries, fathers everywhere have known exactly how he felt.

In a 1955 television interview, Harry Truman commented, "I have always found the best way to give advice to your children is to find out what they want and then advise them to do it." Obviously, President Truman spoke from experience. No matter how sound a father's recommendations may be, almost every child seems compelled to do it "my way."

In this chapter, we consider an assortment of helpful hints that fathers everywhere might be proud to share—and kids everywhere might be likely to ignore.

In our family, we try to make something happen
rather than wait around for it to happen.
—*James Jordan, Michael Jordan's father*

My father is the standard by which all subsequent
men in my life have been judged.
—*Kathryn McCarthy Graham*

Advice is a sacred thing.
—*Plato*

We may give advice, but we cannot inspire conduct.
—*La Rochefoucauld*

My son, hear the instruction of thy father.

—*Proverbs 1:8 KJV*

No one wants advice—only corroboration.

—*John Steinbeck*

Every morning at our house we had squats and sit-ups
15 minutes before breakfast. My father used to say,
"First you have to earn your breakfast."

—*Arnold Schwarzenegger*

The only thing Dad ever told me was to go out and
have fun, stay out of trouble, and be a good kid.

—*Ken Griffey, Jr.*

Bitterness imprisons life, love releases it.

—Harry Emerson Fosdick

Scatter seeds of kindness.

—George Ade

No act of kindness, no matter how small,
is ever wasted.

—Aesop

Look upon the errors of others in sorrow,
not in anger.

—Henry Wadsworth Longfellow

Life is an exercise in forgiveness.

—Norman Cousins

The jealous are troublesome to others but
a torment to themselves.

—*William Penn*

Jealousy is a mental cancer.

—*B. C. Forbes*

Don't lose faith in humanity: Think of all the people
in the United States who have never played
you a single nasty trick.

—*Elbert Hubbard*

The only way to have a friend is to be one.

—*Ralph Waldo Emerson*

If you can't stand yourself, neither can anybody else!

—*Sid Caesar*

People ought to do what comes easy for them.
  Too many struggle with things that are difficult for
  them and that they have no business trying to do.
                                        —*George Bernard Shaw*

Work is a grand cure of all the maladies
            that ever beset mankind.

                                        —*Thomas Carlyle*

Blessed is the man who has found his work.
                                        —*Elbert Hubbard*

People who suffer in unsatisfying jobs are assuming
  the victim role. Nothing is going to help them
          if they don't help themselves.
                                        —*Bernie Siegel, M.D.*

Work and save.

—*Bernard Baruch*

If there is no wind, row.

—*Latin Proverb*

A gentleman never insults anyone intentionally.
Don't look for trouble, but if you get into a fight,
make sure you win it.

—*Clyde Morrison, John Wayne's Father*

The secret of a long life is double careers. One to about
age 60, then another for the next 30 years.

—*David Ogilvy*

Work as if you were to live 100 years;
pray as if you were to die tomorrow.

Ben Franklin

When you're green, you're growing. When you're ripe, you rot.

—

Ray Kroc, the "Father"
of McDonald's Restaurants

Be slow in choosing a friend, slower in changing
a friendship.

—Benjamin Franklin

Never take away hope from any human being.

—Oliver Wendell Holmes, Sr.

One thorn of experience is worth a whole wilderness
of warning.

—James Russell Lowell

Never wait for trouble.

—Charles "Chuck" Yeager

The time will come when winter will ask what you
were doing all summer.

—Henry Clay

Genius is nothing but a greater aptitude for patience.

—Ben Franklin

If you only keep adding little by little,
it will soon become a big heap.

—Hesiod

Here is the test to find whether your mission
on earth is finished: If you're alive, it isn't.

—Richard Bach

All good abides with him who waiteth wisely.

—Henry David Thoreau

No great thing is created suddenly.

—Epictetus

Rudeness is the
weak man's
imitation of strength.

—

Eric Hoffer

You can't hold a man down without staying
down with him.

—*Booker T. Washington*

Conscience is the perfect interpreter of life.

—*Karl Barth*

If you tell the truth, you don't have
to remember anything.

—*Mark Twain*

Every charitable act is a stepping-stone toward heaven.

—*Henry Ward Beecher*

Parenting with Patience

Parenting requires patience. From time to time, even the most mannerly children may do things that worry us, or confuse us, or anger us. Why? Because they are children and because they are human. And, it is precisely *because* they are human that we must, from time to time, be patient with our children's shortcomings (just as they, too, must be patient with ours). Sometimes, patience is the price we pay for being responsible parents, and that's as it should be. After all, think how patient *our* parents have been with us.

Patience and perseverance at length, accomplish more than anger or brute strength.

—

Jean de La Fontaine

Chapter 4
Courage

One man with courage
is a majority.

—

Andrew Jackson

Thoughtful fathers teach the importance of courage and character, knowing that their children will then pass along the message to future generations. But, the teaching process requires more than words; morality lessons, like all paternal preachments, are best taught by example.

Heraclitus observed, "A man's fate is his character." He might have added that a father's character often contributes to the fate of his children. The following quotations remind us that character pays big dividends—now, and for generations to come.

Courage is the first of human qualities because
    it is the quality which guarantees all the others.

—Sir Winston Churchill

Courage is always the surest wisdom.

—Sir Wilfred Grenfell

When there is no money, half is gone;
    when there is no courage, all is gone.

—Old Jewish Saying

Courage is grace under pressure.

—Ernest Hemingway

Nerve succeeds.

—*Old Jewish Saying*

Courage is contagious. When a brave man takes a stand, the spines of others are often stiffened.

—*Billy Graham*

When you're afraid, keep your mind on what you have to do. And if you have been thoroughly prepared, you will not be afraid.

—*Dale Carnegie*

They conquer who believe they can.

—*John Dryden*

Character is that which can do without success.
—*Ralph Waldo Emerson*

Character is what you are in the dark.
—*Dwight L. Moody*

Character is much easier kept than recovered.
—*Thomas Paine*

Character is like the foundation of a house:
It lies beneath the surface and
everything else rests upon it.

—*Anonymous*

Even if fear can act as a good advisor,
there is no use cultivating it.
In the long run it can only hurt you.

—*Luciano Pavarotti*

Fear corrupts.

—*John Steinbeck*

Do the thing you fear and the death of fear is certain.

—*Ralph Waldo Emerson*

Where is the university for courage?
The university for courage is to do
what you believe in!

—*El Cordobés, world-renowned Spanish matador*

Discontent is want of self-reliance.

—*Ralph Waldo Emerson*

We must have courage to bet on our ideas,
to take the calculated risk, and to act.
Everyday living requires courage if life
is to be effective and bring happiness.

—*Maxwell Maltz*

Courage is resistance to fear, mastery of fear—
not absence of fear.

—*Mark Twain*

The only courage that matters is the kind
that gets you from one moment to the next.

—*Mignon McLaughlin*

Parenting with Courage

Being a responsible father is, at times, a daunting task. Raising a family is never easy, but when times are tough, it can be downright frightening. When the storm clouds form overhead, we may find our faith stretched to the breaking point.

As fathers, we must, on occasion, feign courage even when we are afraid. Sometimes, even when we are worried or confused, we must follow the admonition of Robert Louis Stevenson who advised, "Share your courage with others, but keep your fears to yourself."

Are you trying to be a dedicated dad in a difficult world? You've got company. Fathers of this generation—and every one that preceded it—have faced the challenges and responsibilities of protecting and supporting their families. You face those same responsibilities; when you face them with character and courage, your family wins...and so do you.

You don't raise heroes,
you raise sons.
And if you treat them
like sons, they'll turn
out to be heroes,
even if it's just in
your own eyes.

—

Walter M. Schirra, Sr.

Chapter 5
Happiness

A good laugh is sunshine in a house.

—

William Makepeace Thackeray

Fathers seek happiness for their children but cannot force it upon them. Ultimately, each child must bear the responsibility for his own peace of mind—or lack thereof. As Aristotle observed, "Happiness depends upon ourselves."

While you, as a caring father, cannot *force* your children to be happy, you can *prepare them* for happiness by teaching them to live responsibly. If you earnestly desire happiness for your children, teach them discipline, optimism, generosity, honesty, self-reliance, courage, love, and faith. When you do, your children will discover happiness not because you gave it to them but because you taught them how to earn it for themselves.

Happiness comes of the capacity to feel deeply,
to enjoy simply, to think freely,
to risk life, to be needed.

—*Storm Jameson*

Happiness is when what you think, what you say,
and what you do are in harmony.

—*Mohandas Gandhi*

Happiness is something you get as a by-product
in the process of making something else.

—*Aldous Huxley*

Choose a job you love, and you will never work
a day in your life.

—*Confucius*

Mirth is better than fun, and happiness is
better than mirth.

—William Blake

Humor is the best therapy.

—Norman Cousins

An inexhaustible good nature is one
of the most precious gifts of heaven.

—Washington Irving

To live we must conquer incessantly;
we must have the courage to be happy.

—Henri Frédéric Amiel

I am happy and content because I think I am.

—Alain-René Lesage

Happiness is a habit. Cultivate it.

—Elbert Hubbard

Always laugh when you can; it is cheap medicine.
Merriment is a philosophy not well understood.
It is the sunny side of existence.

—George Gordon Byron

A man should so live that his happiness shall depend
as little as possible on external things.

—Epictetus

Happiness depends, as Nature shows,
  Less on exterior things than most suppose.
                                        —*William Cowper*

The U.S. Constitution doesn't guarantee
      happiness, only the pursuit of it.
      You have to catch up with it yourself.
                                        —*Ben Franklin*

Laughter has no foreign accent.
                                        —*Paul Lowney*

To fill the hour and leave no crevice—that is happiness.
                                        —*Ralph Waldo Emerson*

Happiness in this world, when it comes, comes
incidentally. Make it the object of pursuit,
and it leads us on a wild-goose chase
and is never attained. Follow some other object,
and very possibly we may find that we have
caught happiness without dreaming of it.
—*Nathaniel Hawthorne*

Happiness means having something to do
and something to live for.
—*Bishop Fulton J. Sheen*

Happiness to me means constant growth.
—*Eddie Albert*

Humor makes all things tolerable.
—*Henry Ward Beecher*

Don't mistake pleasures for happiness.

—Josh Billings

To do without some of the things you want
is an indispensable part of happiness.

—Bertrand Russell

Be content with such things as ye have.

—Hebrews 13:5

It is right to be contented with what we have,
never with what we are.

—James Mackintosh

Make the work interesting and the discipline
will take care of itself.

—*E. B. White*

Never is work without reward or reward without work.

—*Livy*

I learned from my father how to work.
I learned from him that work is life and
life is work, and work is hard.

—*Philip Roth*

Get happiness out of your work, or you may
never know what happiness is.

—*Elbert Hubbard*

Before we set our hearts too much on anything,
let us examine how happy are those who
already possess it.

—*La Rochefoucauld*

He is the happiest, be he king or peasant,
who finds peace in his home.

—*Goethe*

Everyone chases after happiness, not noticing
that happiness is at their heels.

—*Bertolt Brecht*

The happiness of your life depends upon
the character of your thoughts.

—*Marcus Aurelius*

People with many interests
live not only longest,
but happiest.

—

George Matthew Adams

Encouraging Our Children

Think...pause...then speak: How wise is the father who can communicate in this way. But all too often, in the rush to have themselves heard, fathers may speak first and think later...with unfortunate results.

If we seek to be a source of encouragement to our children, we must measure our words carefully. Words, especially those spoken by a parent, have the power to hurt or to heal. Our words can uplift our children or discourage them. And, of course, if our words are reckless or spoken in haste, they cannot be erased.

As a loving father, your challenge is clear: You must choose words that encourage and empower your children. You must speak wisely, not impulsively. You must employ words of kindness and praise, not words of anger or derision. When you do, you will lift up your children today, and, more importantly, you will give them the confidence they need to lift *themselves* up tomorrow.

The best gift parents
can give children
is themselves.

—

Anonymous

Chapter 6
Faith

The greatest asset of a man,
a business,
or a nation, is faith.

—

Thomas J. Watson

C lement of Alexandria, the Greek theologian, observed, "Faith is the ear of the soul." He might have added that, when it comes to the spiritual ear, most of us suffer from occasional bouts of hearing loss. From time to time, we all fall prey to fits of depression, pessimism or doubt. Even fathers are not immune. But perceptive pops understand that when life gets tough, it's time to turn up the spiritual hearing aid.

No matter how big the problem, faith is the answer. Leo Tolstoy grasped this fact when he wrote, "Faith is the force of life." Hear, hear.

Faith can give us courage to face
the uncertainties of the future.

—*Martin Luther King, Jr.*

Faith is the daring of the soul to go farther than it can see.

—*William Newton Clark*

When you enroll in the "school of faith,"
you never know what may happen next….
The life of faith presents challenges that
keep you going—and keep you growing!

—*Warren Wiersbe*

Treat the other man's faith gently;
it is all he has to believe with.

—*Henry S. Haskins*

Faith means being grasped by a power that
is greater than we are, a power that shakes us and
turns us, and transforms and heals us.
To surrender to this power is faith.

—*Paul Tillich*

Faith is building on what you know is here,
so you can reach what you know is there.

—*Cullen Hightower*

All work that is worth anything is done in faith.

—*Albert Schweitzer*

Belief is a truth held in the mind.
Faith is a fire in the heart.

—*Joseph Fort Newton*

Faith is required of thee, and a sincere life,
        not loftiness of intellect, nor deepness in
            the mysteries of God.

—Thomas à Kempis

Understanding is the reward of faith.
        Therefore seek not to understand
    that thou mayest believe, but believe that thou
        mayest understand.

—St. Augustine

Faith is the substance of things hoped for,
        the evidence of things not seen.

—Hebrews 11:1 KJV

Faith is a higher facility than reason.

—Philip James Bailey

Faith is reason grown courageous.

—*Sherwood Eddy*

Faith is knowing with your heart.

—*N. Richard Nash*

Hope is an adventure, a going forward—
a confident search for a rewarding life.

—*Karl Menninger*

Deep faith eliminates fear.

—*Lech Walesa*

Love is the seed of all hope. It is the enticement to trust,
to risk, to try, to go on.

—*Gloria Gaither*

No faith is our own that we have not arduously won.

—Havelock Ellis

No one is surprised over what God does
when he has faith in Him.

—Oswald Chambers

Entertain great hopes.

—Robert Frost

Hope deferred maketh the heart sick.

—Proverbs 13:12 KJV

Some things have to be believed to be seen.

—Ralph Hodgson

Faith for Today

When the sun is shining and all is well, it's easy to have faith. When the family is at peace, it is easy to feel at peace. When the pantry is full and the bank balance is high, it is easy to be optimistic. But, when life takes an unexpected turn for the worse, as it does on occasion, it is all too easy to lose faith in the future. To do so is a mistake of profound proportions.

During the darker days of life, we must never *abandon* faith; we must, instead, *cultivate* it. We must, without reservation, cultivate faith in ourselves, in our own abilities, and in our God. Then, armed with a faith that is grounded in reality but steeped in possibility, we can summon the courage to face our challenges head-on. When we do, we will be shocked at the power of mountain-moving faith.

And now, with no further ado, let the mountain moving begin.

They can conquer who
believe they can.

—

Ralph Waldo Emerson

Chapter 7
Hard Work

A journey
of a thousand miles
begins with one step.

—

Lao-tzu

The Book of Ecclesiasticus tells us that "Hard work is the lot of every man." It might be added that the lot of most fathers is *very* hard work. But, thoughtful dads don't just bring home the bacon; they teach their children to do the same.

Leonardo da Vinci observed, "God sells us all things at the price of labor." Hard-working fathers understand exactly what Leonardo meant: the key to success is a willingness to pay the price.

Savvy dads know that dreams become reality through the dint of hard work. And the time to get busy is now.

All work is as seed sown; it grows and
spreads and sows itself anew.

—Thomas Carlyle

The world is blessed most by men who do things,
and not by those who merely talk about them.

—James Oliver

Everywhere in life, the true question
is not what we gain, but what we do.

—Thomas Carlyle

Make it a point to do something every day that
you don't want to do. This is the golden rule
for acquiring the habit of doing
your duty without pain.

—Mark Twain

The test of any man lies in action.

—Pindar

Life leaps like a geyser for those who drill through
the rock of inertia.

—Alexis Carrel

For purposes of action, nothing is more useful
than narrowness of thought combined
with energy of will.

—Henri Frédéric Amiel

He who considers too much will perform little.

—Schiller

Knowing is not enough, we must apply;
willing is not enough, we must do.

—Goethe

The great end of life is not knowledge but action.

—*Thomas Huxley*

Shallow men believe in luck. Strong men believe
in cause and effect.

—*Ralph Waldo Emerson*

Dreams pass into reality of action. From the action
stems the dream again; and this interdependence
produces the highest form of living.

—*Anaïs Nin*

The world cares very little about what a man
or woman knows; it is what the man or woman
is able to do that counts.

—*Booker T. Washington*

Our main business is not to see what lies dimly
at a distance, but to do what lies clearly at hand.

—*Thomas Carlyle*

Do noble things, do not dream them all day long.

—*Charles Kingsley*

Everything comes to him who hustles while he waits.

—*Thomas Edison*

To work is to pray.

—*Benedictine Motto*

If you can dream it, you can do it.

—*Walt Disney*

Work and love—these are the basics.

—Theodor Reik

Well done is better than well said.

—Ben Franklin

There is a future that makes itself and a future
that you make. The real future is composed of both.

—Alain

God gives every bird its food, but he does
not throw it into the nest.

—Josiah Gilbert Holland

Live truth instead of professing it.

—Elbert Hubbard

Hell is to drift. Heaven is to steer.

—George Bernard Shaw

Take time to deliberate; but when the time
    for action arrives, stop thinking and go ahead.

—Andrew Jackson

To win one's joy through struggle is better than
    to yield to melancholy.

—André Gide

It is faith, and not reason, which impels men to action.
    Intelligence is content to point out the road
        but never drives us along it.

—Alexis Carrel

To think is easy, to act is difficult;
    to act as one thinks is most difficult of all.

—Goethe

Do what you can with what you have
                where you are.

—Theodore Roosevelt

Elbow grease is the best polish.

—English Proverb

Luck is the residue of design.

—Branch Rickey

You cannot plow a field by turning it over in your mind.

—Anonymous

Do everything. One thing may turn out right.

—Humphrey Bogart

Setting a Worthy Example

We live in a world that is filled to the brim with opportunities to make foolish choices. On the road of life, there exist countless dead ends, detours, and paths that lead far from the straight and narrow course. When we steer away from the path of prudence—and fall short by behaving foolishly or recklessly— we suffer (as do our families). But, when we, as concerned fathers, live honestly and wisely, we become powerful, enduring examples to our children.

The lessons that we teach our children come not from the words we speak but from the lives we live. May we live—and teach—accordingly.

Act well at the moment,
and you have
performed a good action
for all eternity.

—

Johann K. Lavater

Chapter 8
Peace of Mind

Trouble knocked at the door but, hearing a laugh within, hurried away.

—

Poor Richard's Almanac

In the first century before the birth of Jesus, Publilius Syrus noted, "An angry father is most cruel toward himself." These words still apply. When a father loses his temper, he instantly becomes his own worst enemy. Unfortunately, the occasional pressures of fatherhood can make peace of mind an elusive goal, even for the most placid parent.

Peace of mind is a gift we give ourselves. The potential for happiness exists within us, but no force on earth can make us happy against our will. Therefore, questions concerning happiness are best posed to the man in the mirror; he is the man—the only man on earth—who can make us happy.

A thankful heart is not only the greatest
    virtue, but the parent of all other virtues.

—*Cicero*

Thanksgiving invites God to bestow a second benefit.

—*Robert Herrick*

In truth, to attain inner peace, one must be willing
    to pass through the contrary to peace.

—*Swami Brahmananda*

God has two dwellings: one in heaven,
    and the other in a meek and thankful heart.

—*Izaak Walton*

Contentment is a pearl of great price,
    and whoever procures it at the expense of
ten thousand desires makes a wise and happy purchase.

—*John Balguy*

Order your soul; reduce your wants; live in charity;
associate in Christian community; obey the laws;
trust in Providence.

—St. Augustine

If there is to be any peace, it will come
through being, not having.

—Henry Miller

Peace is not the absence of conflict, but the
presence of God no matter what the conflict.

—Anonymous

The peace is won by accompanying God into battle.

—Eivind Berggrav

Little minds have little worries. Big minds
have no room for worries.

—Ralph Waldo Emerson

Sadness is almost never anything but a form of fatigue.

—André Gide

The happiness of man consists in life. And life is labor.

—Leo Tolstoy

How unhappy is he who cannot forgive himself.

—Publilius Syrus

A well-spent day brings happy sleep.

—Leonardo da Vinci

Thinking about interior peace destroys interior peace.
The patient who constantly feels his pulse
is not getting any better.

—Hubert van Zeller

The busiest man is the happiest man.

—*Sir Theodore Martin*

Forgiving those who hurt us is the key to personal peace.

—*G. Weatherly*

Peace is the deepest thing a human personality can know,
it is almighty.

—*Oswald Chambers*

No man is more cheated than the selfish man.

—*Henry Ward Beecher*

When troubles arise, wise men go to their work.

—*Elbert Hubbard*

If we have not peace within ourselves,
    it is in vain to seek it from outward sources.

        —*La Rochefoucauld*

Greatness occurs when your children love you,
    when your critics respect you, and
    when you have peace of mind.

        —*Quincy Jones*

A contented mind is the greatest blessing
    a man can enjoy in this life.

        —*Joseph Addison*

We are not at peace with others because we are not at
    peace with ourselves, and we are not at peace with
    ourselves because we are not at peace with God.

        —*Thomas Merton*

Most folks are about as happy
as they make up their minds to be.

—*Abraham Lincoln*

Contentment consists not in multiplying
wealth but in subtracting desires.

—*Thomas Fuller*

Abundance consists not so much in material
possessions but in an uncovetous spirit.

—*John Selden*

Living well and beautifully and justly are all one thing

—*Socrates*

Only the just man enjoys peace of mind.

—*Epictetus*

Better one hand full and peace of mind,
    than both fists full and toil that is chasing
        the wind.

—Ecclesiastes 4:6

I have learned, in whatever state I am,
    therewith to be content.

—Philippians 4:11

Troubles are often the tools by which God
    fashions us for better things.

—Henry Ward Beecher

There may be those on earth who dress
    better or eat better, but those who enjoy
        the peace of God sleep better.

—L. Thomas Holdcraft

The Joys and Frustrations of Fatherhood

Fatherhood is vastly rewarding, but, as every father knows, it can also be frustrating. No family is perfect, and even the most understanding dad's patience can wear thin on occasion.

When you are tempted to lose your temper over the minor inconveniences of family life, don't. Count to ten, and, if that doesn't work, keep counting. If you find yourself mired in the pit of negativity, take time for a much-needed pit stop. As you slow down to gather your emotions, turn your thoughts to the blessings and the love that *have* come and *will* come from the family that calls you "Dad." And how many blessings should you count? Count to ten, and, if that doesn't work, keep counting.

A man travels the world over in search of what he needs and returns home to find it.

—

George Moore

Chapter 9
Life

Life is 10% what you make it and 90% how you take it.

—

Irving Berlin

Henry James once advised, "Live all you can; it's a mistake not to. It doesn't so much matter what you do, so long as you have your life. If you haven't had that, what have you had?"

A father's job is to help his children understand that life should be savored, not squandered. It was Bishop Fulton J. Sheen who observed, "Time is so precious that God deals it out only second by second." This earthly life is, indeed, a brief interval between birth and death. Our challenge, of course, is to determine how best to use it...and to teach our children to do the same.

One life—a little gleam of time between two eternities.
—*Thomas Carlyle*

Is not life a hundred times too short for us
to bore ourselves?
—*Friedrich Nietzsche*

There are two lasting bequests we can hope
to give our children. One of these is roots;
the other, wings.
—*Hodding Carter*

Real generosity toward the future consists
in giving all to what is present.
—*Albert Camus*

Life is what happens to us while we are
                making other plans.

—Thomas La Mance

Everyone's life is a fairy tale written by God's fingers.

—Hans Christian Andersen

Life is not a problem to be solved
                but a reality to be experienced.

—Søren Kierkegaard

Life is like playing a violin in public
                and learning the instrument as one goes on.

—Samuel Butler

Life is a series of collisions with the future;
                it is not a sum of what we have been
                        but what we yearn to be.

—José Ortega y Gasset

Life can only be understood backwards
         but must be lived forward.

                                          —Søren Kierkegaard

When you were born, you cried and the world rejoiced!
    Live your life in such a manner that when you die,
        the world cries and you rejoice.

                                          —Old Indian Saying

Life is a great bundle of little things.

                                        —Oliver Wendell Holmes, Sr.

The present will not long endure.

                                        —Pindar

Growth is the only evidence of life.

                                    —John Henry Cardinal Newman

Life is a language in which certain truths are conveyed
to us; if we could learn them in some other way,
we should not live.

—*Arthur Schopenhauer*

The great use of life is to spend it
for something that will outlast it.

—*William James*

As I grow to understand life less and less,
I learn to live it more and more.

—*Jules Renard*

Life ain't no dress rehearsal!

—*Mark Twain*

Life is the art of drawing sufficient conclusions
from insufficient premises.

—*Samuel Butler*

Life is like a game of cards. The hand that is dealt
you represents determinism;
the way you play it is free will.

—*Jawaharlal Nehru*

The game of life is not so much in holding
a good hand as playing a poor hand well.

—*H. T. Leslie*

Our life is what our thoughts make it.

—*Marcus Aurelius*

Tell me whom you love, and
I will tell you what you are.

—*Arsène Houssaye*

Life is a romantic business,
but you have to make the romance.

—*Oliver Wendell Holmes, Sr.*

If you want to die happily, learn to live.

—*Celio Calcagnini*

Life is the flower of which love is the honey.

—*Victor Hugo*

Passion makes all things alive and significant.

—*Ralph Waldo Emerson*

We have no more right to consume happiness
without producing it than to consume
wealth without producing it.

—George Bernard Shaw

He only is advancing in life whose heart is
getting softer, whose blood warmer,
whose brain quicker, whose spirit
is entering into living peace.

—John Ruskin

To live is not to live for one's self alone;
let us help one another.

—Menander

When people are serving,
life is no longer meaningless.

—John Gardner

The man who has no inner life is the slave
of his surroundings.

—*Henri Frédéric Amiel*

Every man's life is a plan of God.

—*Horace Bushnell*

He who has a "why" to live for can bear
with almost any "how."

—*Friedrich Nietzsche*

Life is short. Make the most of the present.

—*Marcus Aurelius*

The best way to
prepare for life
is to begin to live.

—

Elbert Hubbard

Celebrating Today

The 118th Psalm reminds us "This is the day which the Lord hath made; we will rejoice and be glad in it." As we rejoice in this day that the Lord has given, let us remember that an important part of today's celebration is the time we spend offering thanks. Each new dawn breaks upon a day filled with countless possibilities. To forget to say "Thank You" for these gifts is not simply poor manners, it is also sloppy thinking.

Today and every day therafter, let's give thanks for this opportunity called life. Even if the day holds a few unpleasant moments (as most days do), let us be thankful for the good times (which, for most of us, far outnumber the bad). Let's look for the good in others (starting with our families), and let us celebrate the good that we find. When we begin to search for reasons to celebrate the gift of life, we find them all around us...starting with those good people who live under the roof of the house we call home.

Thank God every morning
when you get up that
you have something to do
that day which must be
done, whether you
like it or not.

—

Charles Kingsley

Chapter 10
Success

It takes twenty years
to make an overnight
success.

—

Eddie Cantor

Phillips Brooks observed, "To find his place and fill it is success for a man." But finding one's place is not always easy. Sometimes, a little fatherly advice can help.

The British writer George Bernard Shaw defined success by saying, "This is the true joy in life: being used for a purpose recognized by yourself as a mighty one." If you're interested in ways to recognize *your* place and successfully fill it, read on. The following quotations provide advice that any father would be proud to call his own.

The destiny of man is in his own soul.

—Herodotus

Success is simple. Do what's right, the right way,
at the right time.

—Arnold Glasow

Success abides longer among men
when it is planted by the hand of God.

—Pindar

He who would climb the ladder must begin
at the bottom.

—English Proverb

You always pass failure on the way to success.

—Mickey Rooney

It takes time to be a good father. It takes effort trying,
failing, and trying again.

—Tim Hansel

Why should we be in such desperate haste to succeed,
and in such desperate enterprises? If a man does not keep
pace with his companions, perhaps it is because
he hears a different drummer.

—Henry David Thoreau

Being humble involves the willingness to be reckoned
a failure in everyone's sight but God's.

—Roy M. Pearson

Success is to be measured not by wealth, power,
or fame, but by the ratio between what
a man is and what he might be.

—H. G. Wells

Work to become, not to acquire.

—*Elbert Hubbard*

He who has never failed somewhere,
            that man cannot be great.

—*Herman Melville*

There is no failure except in no longer trying.

—*Elbert Hubbard*

Failure is only the opportunity to begin again,
            more intelligently.

—*Henry Ford*

The way to success is to double your failure rate.

—*Thomas J. Watson*

It is hard to fail, but it is worse never to have
tried to succeed.

—Theodore Roosevelt

When you blunder, blunder forward.

—Thomas Edison

Constant effort and frequent mistakes
are the stepping-stones of genius.

—Elbert Hubbard

How to succeed—try hard enough.
How to fail—try too hard.

—Malcolm Forbes

Whatever you do, do it with purpose;
    do it thoroughly, not superficially.

—*Lord Chesterfield*

Success consists in the climb.

—*Elbert Hubbard*

If you wish to succeed in life, make perseverance
    your bosom friend, experience your wise counselor,
        caution your elder brother, and
            hope your guardian genius.

—*Joseph Addison*

Show class, have pride, and display character.
    If you do, winning will take care of itself.

—*Bear Bryant*

If A equals success, then the formula is
    A equals X plus Y plus Z. X is work. Y is play.
        Z is keep your mouth shut.

—*Albert Einstein*

The secret to success in life is for a man to
    be ready for his opportunity when it comes.

—*Benjamin Disraeli*

To be successful, a certain single-mindedness
        is required—on the court or off.

—*Arthur Ashe*

I can give you a six-word formula for success:
    Think things through—then follow through.

—*Eddie Rickenbacker*

Great minds have purposes,
        others have wishes.

                          —Washington Irving

The man without a purpose is like a ship
        without a rudder—a waif, a nothing,
                a no man.

                          —Thomas Carlyle

Try not to become a man of success
        but rather a man of value.

                          —Albert Einstein

Life offers no assurances, so you might as
        well do what you're really passionate about.

                          —Jim Carrey

Whenever you see a successful business,
    someone once made a courageous decision.

—Peter Drucker

Do your work with your whole heart, and you
    will succeed—there is so little competition.

—Elbert Hubbard

The secret of success is constancy of purpose.

—Benjamin Disraeli

Einstein's three rules of work:
1. Out of clutter find simplicity.
2. From discord make harmony.
3. In the middle of difficulty lies opportunity.

I look on that man as happy who,
when there is question of success,
looks to his work for a reply.

—*Ralph Waldo Emerson*

Success is relative. It is what we can make
of the mess we have made of things.

—*T. S. Eliot*

Success has nothing to do with what you gain
in life or accomplish for yourself.
It is what you do for others.

—*Danny Thomas*

Living With a Purpose

Life is best lived on purpose. Unfortunately, too many of us begin each day without a clear idea of what we wish to accomplish...or why.

If you cannot lay your hands on a clear, concise version of your own personal mission statement, put down this book, grab a pen and paper, and start writing. Then, once you've clearly established what you wish to make of your life, get busy making it. And, while you're at it, teach your children to do likewise.

Human lives, like sailing ships, function best with maps and rudders. As you sail your own little ship on the seas of life, the map you use should be one of your own creation, and the rudder by which you steer should be placed firmly in the control of your own hand. Otherwise, you are not really sailing your own ship at all...you're simply cargo on someone else's boat. Resolve, therefore, to be the captain of your own vessel. And then, with your map in full view and your course clearly set, it's time to set sail...and live.

Success is finishing
what God gave
you to do.

—

Harold Cook

Chapter 11
Memories

It doesn't matter who
my father was; it matters
who I remember he was.

—

Anne Sexton

Memories of our fathers are priceless possessions; in this chapter, a few notable figures share theirs. Republican Howard Baker once observed, "My father had a profound impact on me in a way I don't think I could ever explain." Democrat Mario Cuomo remembered his father by saying, "I talk and talk and talk, and I haven't taught people in 50 years what my father taught by example in one week." Mr. Baker and Mr. Cuomo thus proved once and for all that admiration for our fathers is something upon which even Republicans and Democrats can agree.

Growing up as a preacher's son was tough because
the other kids figured you had money.
We didn't. What we did have was a daddy
with tremendous integrity, a genuine Christian,
and a mother with boundless love.

—*Sinbad*

My father had the poorest lemon ranch in California,
I can assure you. He sold it before they found oil on it.

—*Richard M. Nixon*

My father was not a failure. After all, he was the father
of a president of the United States.

—*Harry S. Truman*

My parents were strict, disciplined, and oriented
toward education. My father worked very hard
to build a good life for us. My mother loved
to cook and work and laugh.

—*José Canseco*

I had a wonderful, happy childhood. I think my parents
liked to inspire creativity, winningness, productivity
in their children. It mattered to them what
we thought, felt, and did. Our happiness was
important to them.

—*John Travolta*

Pop didn't just teach me golf. He taught me discipline.

—*Arnold Palmer*

When my mother needed someone 24 years ago,
Phil Harrison was the man. He is my dad.
He's the one who raised me and made me
what I am today.

—*Shaquille O'Neal, on his stepfather*

My father produced Shakespeare festivals throughout
Ohio when I was growing up. I played more
murdered princes, mustard seeds, and fairies
and elves than I could count.

—*John Lithgow*

It's hard for me to talk about a legacy or a mystique.
It's my family—the fact that there have been
difficulties and hardships makes us closer.

—*John F. Kennedy, Jr.*

I never thought of us as rich or poor. We always had
enough. We never had a car and we didn't have a radio.
My father's little motorbike was the family
transportation. I never thought about what
we didn't have; I am still that way. All around me
I see people making themselves unhappy
with such thoughts.

—*Luciano Pavarotti*

Our father, while he lived, had cast a magic over
everything. He held his love up over us like
an umbrella and kept off the troubles.

—*Mary Lavin*

I watched a small man with thick calluses on
both hands work 15 to 16 hours a day. I saw him
once literally bleed from the bottoms of his feet,
a man who came here uneducated, alone, unable
to speak the language, who taught me all I needed
to know about faith and hard work by
the simple eloquence of his example.

—*Mario Cuomo*

He was a man who for years had, to my naturally
prejudiced mind, set a splendid example—not just
to me but to the world—of irresistible optimism
and vitality, and a love of all that life could offer.

—*Douglas Fairbanks, Jr.*

Everyone had their chores. We all had to eat together
every meal. Mom cooked, we helped,
while we waited for Dad to come home
from work. It was like the American Dream.
My family was almost perfect. I was very lucky.

—*Reggie Miller*

My father saved my life.

—*Oprah Winfrey*

The imprint of the parent remains forever
on the life of the child.

—*C. B. Eavey*

He was a gentleman and a gentle man.
My father was sweet, kind, and good-hearted.
He loved his family and spent as much time
as he could with us.

—*Natalie Cole, on her father Nat King Cole*

He gave me some valuable things: he gave me
　　fighting blood, which I needed.

—*Tennessee Williams*

I wanted to be like my father, but not *exactly* like him.
　　It's tough growing up in the shadow
　　　of a national monument.

—*Jane Fonda*

I don't think I've been a particularly good father,
　　but I've been lucky in the quality of my kids.

—*Henry Fonda*

When a child, my dreams rode on your wishes,
　　I was your son, high on your horse,
　　My mind atop whipped by the lashes
　　Of your rhetoric, windy of course.

—*Stephen Foster*

Pride in one's father reinforces love.

—

Margaret Truman

And finally,
a word of advice
for children of all ages...

Honor thy father and thy mother.

—

Exodus 20:12 KJV

About the Author

Criswell Freeman is a Doctor of Clinical Psychology living in Nashville, Tennessee. He is the author of *When Life Throws You a Curveball, Hit It* and numerous books in the Wisdom Series published by WALNUT GROVE PRESS.

Dr. Freeman's Wisdom Books chronicle memorable quotations in an easy-to-read style. The series provides inspiring, thoughtful and humorous messages from entertainers, athletes, scientists, politicians, clerics, writers and renegades. Combining his passion for quotations with extensive training in psychology, Freeman revisits timeless themes such as perseverance, courage, love, forgiveness and faith.

Dr. Freeman is also the host of *Wisdom Made in America*, a nationally syndicated radio program.